KIDS'

BIBLE
TRIVIA

Paul Kent

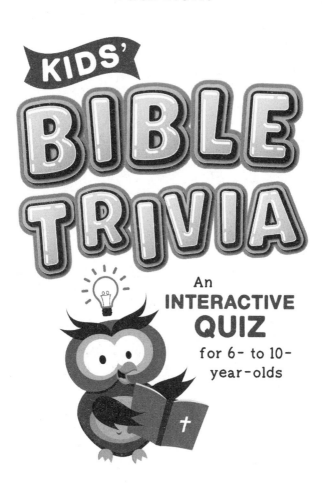

KIDS' BIBLE TRIVIA

An
**INTERACTIVE
QUIZ**
for 6- to 10-
year-olds

BARBOUR **kidz**
A Division of Barbour Publishing

© 2002 by Barbour Publishing, Inc.

Previously published as *My Final Answer for Kids*

ISBN 978-1-63609-360-4

Scripture taken from the Holy Bible, New International Version®. niv®. Copyright © 1973, 1978, 1984, 2011 by Biblica, Inc.™ Used by permission. All rights reserved worldwide.

Published by Barbour Publishing, Inc., 1810 Barbour Drive, Uhrichsville, Ohio 44683, www.barbourbooks.com

Our mission is to inspire the world with the life-changing message of the Bible.

Printed in the United States of America.

001545 0223 BP

CONTENTS

KIDS' BIBLE TRIVIA

An Interactive Quiz for 6–10-Year-Olds

Hey kids—how much do you *really* know about the Bible? Find out here in twenty fun and fascinating quizzes!

Each quiz has six levels of multiple-choice questions, beginning with some really easy stuff. . .you know, the kind of things you learned back in toddler church. But the questions get harder as you move up through the levels.

If you can get through the first two questions without a miss, you'll win Bible Bronze. If you can answer four questions correctly, you'll earn Bible Silver. And if you have the smarts to complete all six questions without a wrong answer, you'll win Bible Gold!

But watch out—you'll have to know your Bible stories awfully well to answer those higher-level questions.

You will have help though. Once in each quiz, you can

x2 Double Your Chances: Look up this bonus to learn two of the wrong answers, or

✝ Look in the Book: Look up this bonus for the question's Bible reference. . . then find your answer in the Good Book itself!

Remember—you get a total of two Bible Bonuses (one of each) in each six-question quiz. The answer to each question is on the following page. . .along with some fun "Did You Know?" questions.

So how much do you *really* know about the Bible? Step up to the microphone and show off your smarts. It's interesting, it's fun, it's *Kids' Bible Trivia*!

QUIZ 1

LEVEL 1

Where did the prophet Jonah spend three strange days and nights?

    a) on a space ship

    b) in an eagle's nest

    c) under a waterfall

    d) inside a fish

Look in the Book: Jonah 1:17

×2 Double Your Chances: A and C

Where did the prophet Jonah spend three strange days and nights?

    a) on a space ship

    b) in an eagle's nest

    c) under a waterfall

    d) inside a fish

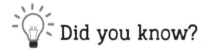 Did you know?

Jesus once said that He would be like Jonah: "As Jonah was three days and three nights in the belly of a huge fish, so the Son of Man will be three days and three nights in the heart of the earth" (Matthew 12:40). Jesus was talking about the time He would be killed and put in a tomb, but three days later come back to life.

BIBLE BRONZE

What were Peter and Andrew doing when Jesus asked them to be His disciples?

a) playing chess

b) building a house

c) fishing

d) cooking dinner

Look in the Book: Matthew 4:18-19

 Double Your Chances: A and D

What were Peter and Andrew doing when Jesus asked them to be His disciples?

  a) playing chess

  b) building a house

  c) fishing

  d) cooking dinner

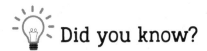 ## Did you know?

Jesus said the famous words "I will make you fishers of men" to Peter and Andrew.

What famous man was the brother of the Old Testament priest Aaron?

 a) Moses

 b) Abraham

 c) Joseph

 d) Adam

Look in the Book: Exodus 4:14

Double Your Chances: B and C

What famous man was the brother of the Old Testament priest Aaron?

a) Moses

b) Abraham

c) Joseph

d) Adam

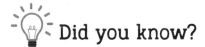 Did you know?

Moses didn't like his own voice—so God said that Aaron would speak for Moses. Look it up in Exodus 6:28–7:2.

BIBLE SILVER

What color horse does Jesus ride during the great battle in the book of Revelation?

> a) gold
>
> b) red
>
> c) white
>
> d) black

 Look in the Book: Revelation 19:11

 Double Your Chances: B and D

What color horse does Jesus ride during the great battle in the book of Revelation?

    a) gold

    b) red

    c) white

    d) black

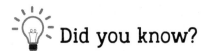 **Did you know?**

The color white stands for things that are pure—like God and Jesus. Daniel says God's clothing is "white as snow," and His hair "white like wool" (Daniel 7:9). In Revelation 20:11, God sits on a "great white throne."

LEVEL 5

Who is Michael in the New Testament?

a) a disciple of Jesus

b) a Roman governor

c) an archangel

d) the author of Galatians

Look in the Book: Jude 9

Double Your Chances: A and D

Who is Michael in the New Testament?

    a) a disciple of Jesus

    b) a Roman governor

    c) an archangel

    d) the author of Galatians

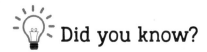 Did you know?

The word *arch* can mean "the most important" —so an *archangel* is "the most important angel."

BIBLE GOLD

Who was stoned to death as the first person to be killed for following Jesus?

a) John

b) James

c) Philip

d) Stephen

Double Your Chances: B and C

Look in the Book: Acts 7:59-60

Who was stoned to death as the first person to be killed for following Jesus?

a) John

b) James

c) Philip

d) Stephen

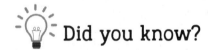 Did you know?

A person who is killed for following Jesus is called a *martyr*.

QUIZ 2

LEVEL 1

How did God destroy the wicked people of the earth during Noah's time?

a) with a giant tornado

b) with a giant fire

c) with a giant flood

d) with a giant

Look in the Book: Genesis 7:17–22

Double Your Chances: B and D

How did God destroy the wicked people of the earth during Noah's time?

    a) with a giant tornado

    b) with a giant fire

    c) with a giant flood

    d) with a giant

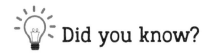 **Did you know?**

Jesus said that His second coming will be like the flood of Noah's time. "In the days before the flood," Jesus said, "people were eating and drinking, marrying and giving in marriage, up to the day Noah entered the ark; and they knew nothing about what would happen until the flood came and took them all away. That is how it will be at the coming of the Son of Man" (Matthew 24:38–39).

BIBLE BRONZE

What kind of tree did Zacchaeus climb in order to see Jesus?

    a) palm

    b) oak

    c) sycamore

    d) crab apple

 Look in the Book: Luke 19:4

 Double Your Chances: A and D

What kind of tree did Zacchaeus climb in order to see Jesus?

    a) palm

    b) oak

    c) sycamore

    d) crab apple

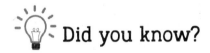 **Did you know?**

God gave His people, the Israelites, some special rules about trees. When the people of Israel were fighting against a city, God told them, "Do not destroy its trees by putting an ax to them, because you can eat their fruit. Do not cut them down. Are the trees people, that you should besiege them?" (Deuteronomy 20:19).

LEVEL 3

What is Methuselah famous for?

a) He was Adam and Eve's favorite
   movie star.

b) He was thrown into the fiery
   furnace.

c) He was brought back to life by
   Elijah.

d) He lived 969 years.

 Look in the Book: Genesis 5:27

 Double Your Chances: A and B

What is Methuselah famous for?

  a) He was Adam and Eve's favorite
     movie star.

  b) He was thrown into the fiery
     furnace.

  c) He was brought back to life by
     Elijah.

  d) He lived 969 years.

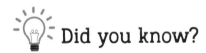 Did you know?

The Guinness Book of World Records says the oldest person in recent times was Jeanne Calment of France. When she died in 1997, she was 122 years old!

What did Jesus say His care for Christians would be like?

a) a man with his son

b) a shepherd with his sheep

c) a king with his queen

d) a bear with her cub

 Look in the Book: John 10:14

 Double Your Chances: C and D

What did Jesus say His care for Christians would be like?

    a) a man with his son

    b) a shepherd with his sheep

    c) a king with his queen

    d) a bear with her cub

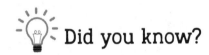 Did you know?

Jesus said a good shepherd knows all of his sheep by name, and the sheep know their shepherd's voice (John 10:3-4)—and that's just like Jesus with His followers!

LEVEL 5

Which disciple said he needed
proof to believe that Jesus
had come back to life?

a) Thomas

b) John

c) Simon the Zealot

d) Peter

Look in the Book: John 20:24-25

Double Your Chances: B and C

Which disciple said he needed
proof to believe that Jesus
had come back to life?

    a) Thomas

    b) John

    c) Simon the Zealot

    d) Peter

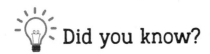 **Did you know?**

The nickname "Doubting Thomas" comes
from this disciple!

BIBLE GOLD

How many years did Jacob agree to work to have Rachel as his wife?

    a) 1

    b) 7

    c) 20

    d) 100

 Look in the Book: Genesis 29:18

 Double Your Chances: C and D

How many years did Jacob agree to work to have Rachel as his wife?

    a) 1

    b) 7

    c) 20

    d) 100

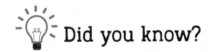 **Did you know?**

Jacob agreed to work seven years for Rachel, but ended up working *fourteen* years for her— because Rachel's father tricked Jacob into marrying Rachel's older sister first. Check out the whole story in Genesis 29:10–30.

QUIZ 3

LEVEL 1

What huge man lost a fight
with a boy named David?

- a) Ishbi-Benob

- b) Goliath

- c) Saph

- d) The Jolly Green Giant

 Double Your Chances: A and D

 Look in the Book: 1 Samuel 17:4, 50

What huge man lost a fight
with a boy named David?

    a) Ishbi-Benob

    b) Goliath

    c) Saph

    d) The Jolly Green Giant

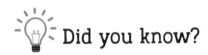 **Did you know?**

Goliath wasn't the only giant bad guy of the
Bible. . .check out 2 Samuel 21:15–22 for
details on some others—including a guy with
twenty-four fingers and toes!

BIBLE BRONZE

What king was known around
the world for his wisdom?

      a) Solomon

      b) Nebuchadnezzar

      c) Agrippa

      d) Burger King

 Look in the Book! 1 Kings 4:29-34

 Double Your Chances: C and D

What king was known around the world for his wisdom?

a) Solomon

b) Nebuchadnezzar

c) Agrippa

d) Burger King

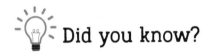 Did you know?

Solomon was also a science teacher! In 1 Kings 4:33, the Bible says he "spoke about plant life, from the cedar of Lebanon to the hyssop that grows out of walls. He also spoke about animals and birds, reptiles and fish." Solomon was so interesting that people came from all over the world to listen to him.

LEVEL 3

What is the name for the stories Jesus told to teach people about God's kingdom?

    a) miracles

    b) parables

    c) oracles

    d) Lunchables

 Look in the Book: Matthew 13:34

Double Your Chances: A and D

What is the name for the stories
Jesus told to teach people about
God's kingdom?

   a) miracles

   b) parables

   c) oracles

   d) Lunchables

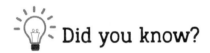 Did you know?

Jesus' story about the Good Samaritan (Luke
10:30–37) was a parable.

What physical problem was the brave army commander Naaman healed of?

    a) blindness

    b) leprosy

    c) fever

    d) a hunched back

Look in the Book: 2 Kings 5:1, 14

Double Your Chances: C and D

What physical problem was the brave army commander Naaman healed of?

a) blindness

b) leprosy

c) fever

d) a hunched back

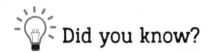 Did you know?

Most people think of leprosy as a disease of the skin—but it can also mess up the lungs and even cause blindness.

LEVEL 5

What did the people of Malta say about the apostle Paul when a snakebite didn't kill him?

    a) that he was lucky

    b) that he was a demon

    c) that he was a god

    d) that he was really tough

 Look in the Book: Acts 28:6

 Double Your Chances: B and D

What did the people of Malta
say about the apostle Paul when
a snakebite didn't kill him?

    a) that he was lucky

    b) that he was a demon

    c) that he was a god

    d) that he was really tough

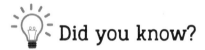 Did you know?

Malta is an island in the Mediterranean Sea. . .
and it has a place called "St. Paul's Bay."

BIBLE GOLD

Which of these women
was a judge of Israel?

      a) Deborah

      b) Bathsheba

      c) Esther

      d) Rebekah

Look in the Book: Judges 4:4

 Double Your Chances: B and C

Which of these women
was a judge of Israel?

a) Deborah

b) Bathsheba

c) Esther

d) Rebekah

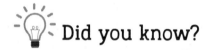 Did you know?

Deborah was also a leader in the army! She
went into battle with a nervous commander
named Barak, who told her, "If you go with
me, I will go; but if you don't go with me, I
won't go" (Judges 4:8).

QUIZ 4

LEVEL 1

What did Adam name his wife?

- a) Madam
- b) Abigail
- c) Mary
- d) Eve

 Double Your Chances: A and B

 Look in the Book: Genesis 3:20

What did Adam name his wife?

    a) Madam

    b) Abigail

    c) Mary

    d) Eve

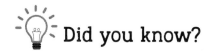 ## Did you know?

Eve means "living."

BIBLE BRONZE

How many criminals were crucified with Jesus?

    a) none

    b) 1

    c) 2

    d) a dozen

Look in the Book: Luke 23:32

Double Your Chances: A and D

How many criminals were crucified with Jesus?

a) none

b) 1

c) 2

d) a dozen

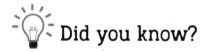 Did you know?

Jesus was crucified at the place called "Calvary." Be careful that you don't say "cavalry"—that's the part of an army that rides horses or trucks into battle!

LEVEL 3

What country suffered ten terrible plagues for keeping God's special people—the Israelites—as slaves?

    a) Egypt

    b) Babylon

    c) Syria

    d) Russia

 Look in the Book: Exodus 7:5

 Double Your Chances: C and D

What country suffered ten terrible plagues for keeping God's special people—the Israelites—as slaves?

a) Egypt

b) Babylon

c) Syria

d) Russia

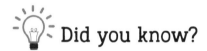 Did you know?

Years before the plagues, Egypt had invited the Israelites to move in—because Egypt's ruler at that time, Joseph, was an Israelite. But later, a new king, "to whom Joseph meant nothing" (Exodus 1:8), took over in Egypt, and made life hard for the Israelites.

BIBLE SILVER

How did Jacob describe
his brother Esau?

    a) scary

    b) wary

    c) hairy

    d) merry

 Look in the Book: Genesis 27:11

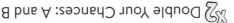 Double Your Chances: A and B

How did Jacob describe
his brother Esau?

  a) scary

  b) wary

  c) hairy

  d) merry

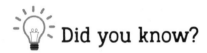 **Did you know?**

Esau was so hairy that his brother Jacob put on
a goat skin to imitate him. Their blind father,
Isaac, felt all of that goat fur and believed that
Jacob, who had smooth skin, was really the
hairy Esau! Read the whole story in Genesis
27:15–23.

What did Jesus drink while
he was on the cross?

a) vinegar

b) milk

c) water

d) olive oil

Look in the Book: John 19:29-30

Double Your Chances: B and D

What did Jesus drink while
he was on the cross?

    a) vinegar

    b) milk

    c) water

    d) olive oil

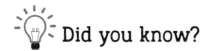 **Did you know?**

Grapes, rice, and other foods can be used to
make vinegar.

What made King Saul stand out from the rest of the Israelites?

    a) He was stronger.

    b) He had darker skin.

    c) He was taller.

    d) He had a nicer voice.

 Look in the Book: 1 Samuel 9:2

 Double Your Chances: B and D

What made King Saul stand out from the rest of the Israelites?

  a) He was stronger.

  b) He had darker skin.

  c) He was taller.

  d) He had a nicer voice.

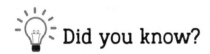 **Did you know?**

Saul was the very first king of Israel—about one thousand years before Jesus was born.

QUIZ 5

LEVEL 1

What miracle did Jesus do for His friend Lazarus?

    a) brought him back to life

    b) turned a stone into bread

    c) healed him of leprosy

    d) turned his spinach into ice cream

 Look in the Book: John 11:43-44

 Double Your Chances: C and D

What miracle did Jesus do
for His friend Lazarus?

a) brought him back to life

b) turned a stone into bread

c) healed him of leprosy

d) turned his spinach into ice cream

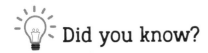 Did you know?

The shortest verse in the Bible is found in the
story of Lazarus. John 11:35 says that when He
saw people crying over Lazarus, "Jesus wept."

BIBLE BRONZE

What did the people of Babel try to build to reach the heavens?

    a) a rocket

    b) a ladder

    c) a staircase

    d) a tower

 Look in the Book: Genesis 11:1–9

 Double Your Chances: A and C

What did the people of Babel try
to build to reach the heavens?

      a) a rocket

      b) a ladder

      c) a staircase

      d) a tower

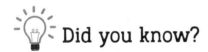 **Did you know?**

The tallest building in the United States is the
One World Trade Center in New York City.
It's more than a quarter of a mile high. . .
but it doesn't reach to heaven!

LEVEL 3

What happened when Jesus
sent demons out of a man
and into a herd of pigs?

a) The pigs fought each other.

b) The pigs began to talk.

c) The pigs ran into a lake and
   drowned.

d) The pigs burst into flames.

Double Your Chances: B and D

Look in the Book: Mark 5:11–13

What happened when Jesus
sent demons out of a man
and into a herd of pigs?

> a) The pigs fought each other.
>
> b) The pigs began to talk.
>
> **c) The pigs ran into a lake and
>   drowned.**
>
> d) The pigs burst into flames.

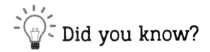 Did you know?

The people of Israel weren't allowed to
eat ham or bacon or pork chops—anything
that came from pigs. God had told them, in
Leviticus 11:7–8, "The pig. . .is unclean for you.
You must not eat their meat."

BIBLE SILVER

What did Jesus use to get Saul's attention on the road to Damascus?

  a) a bright light

  b) a whirlwind

  c) an earthquake

  d) a stampede of elephants

 Look in the Book: Acts 9:3-4

 Double Your Chances: B and D

What did Jesus use to get Saul's attention on the road to Damascus?

a) a bright light

b) a whirlwind

c) an earthquake

d) a stampede of elephants

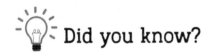 **Did you know?**

Saul was on his way to *arrest* Christians, when God turned Saul himself into a Christian! Later, Saul was called "Paul" and wrote several of the books of the New Testament.

LEVEL 5

What strange vision did
Ezekiel once have?

      a) a tree in the middle of a tree

      b) a box in the middle of a box

      c) a wheel in the middle of a wheel

      d) a star in the middle of a star

 Look in the Book: Ezekiel 1:16

 Double Your Chances: A and B

What strange vision did
Ezekiel once have?

    a) a tree in the middle of a tree

    b) a box in the middle of a box

    c) a wheel in the middle of a wheel

    d) a star in the middle of a star

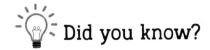 Did you know?

Ezekiel had another strange vision, of a valley
full of dried up bones (Ezekiel 37:1–10). God
told Ezekiel to speak to the bones, and they
came together into skeletons, grew skin, and
came back to life. Weird, huh?

BIBLE GOLD

What was Judas Iscariot's pay for betraying Jesus?

    a) two new coats

    b) five bulls

    c) twelve swords

    d) thirty silver coins

 Look in the Book: Matthew 26:14–15

 Double Your Chances: B and C

What was Judas Iscariot's pay
for betraying Jesus?

    a) two new coats

    b) five bulls

    c) twelve swords

    d) thirty silver coins

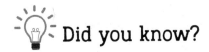 Did you know?

After Jesus had been arrested and sentenced
to death, Judas felt guilty about what he had
done and tried to give the money back. Then
he went out and killed himself. See for yourself in Matthew 27:3–5.

QUIZ 6

LEVEL 1

What gifts did the wise men bring to the young child Jesus?

    a) gold, frankincense, and myrrh

    b) silver, soap, and sandals

    c) honey, cheese, and nuts

    d) baseballs, footballs, and hockey sticks

Look in the Book: Matthew 2:11

Double Your Chances: B and D

Kids' Bible Trivia

What gifts did the wise men bring
to the young child Jesus?

a) gold, frankincense, and myrrh

b) silver, soap, and sandals

c) honey, cheese, and nuts

d) baseballs, footballs, and hockey
   sticks

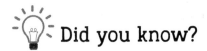 Did you know?

Well, you already know what gold is. . .but
frankincense and myrrh are things that smell
good!

BIBLE BRONZE

What man's wife turned into a pillar of salt after disobeying God?

    a) Lot

    b) Moses

    c) Peter

    d) Joe Biden

 Look in the Book: Genesis 19:26

 Double Your Chances: B and D

What man's wife turned into a pillar of salt after disobeying God?

    a) Lot

    b) Moses

    c) Peter

    d) Joe Biden

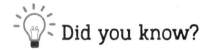 Did you know?

Lot had an uncle named Abraham. . .who started the nation that would be called "Israel."

LEVEL 3

What kind of animal spoke to
a prophet named Balaam?

    a) a platypus

    b) a dog

    c) a lion

    d) a donkey

 Look in the Book: Numbers 22:28

Double Your Chances: A and B

What kind of animal spoke to
a prophet named Balaam?

> a) a platypus
>
> b) a dog
>
> c) a lion
>
> **d) a donkey**

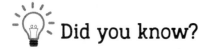 Did you know?

One of the judges of Israel, a man named Jair,
had thirty sons. . .who rode thirty donkeys
(Judges 10:3–4)!

What did the Holy Spirit look like when it came down on Jesus after His baptism?

a) a dove

b) a cloud

c) a hawk

d) lightning

Look in the Book: Luke 3:21–22

Double Your Chances: B and C

What did the Holy Spirit look like when it came down on Jesus after His baptism?

a) a dove

b) a cloud

c) a hawk

d) lightning

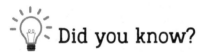 **Did you know?**

Jesus once told His disciples to be "as shrewd [smart] as snakes and as innocent as doves" (Matthew 10:16).

LEVEL 5

Who was Solomon's father?

a) Adam

b) Daniel

c) Nehemiah

d) David

 Look in the Book: 2 Samuel 12:24

Double Your Chances: A and C

Who was Solomon's father?

    a) Adam

    b) Daniel

    c) Nehemiah

    d) David

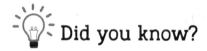 Did you know?

David and Solomon were both ancestors (early relatives) of Jesus. In Matthew 1:1, Jesus is even called the "Son of David," which means that He is an important relative of Israel's great king.

BIBLE GOLD

Which of Jesus' twelve disciples
was the brother of John?

a) Judas Iscariot

b) Andrew

c) Matthew

d) James

 Look in the Book: Mark 3:17

 Double Your Chances: A and B

79

Which of Jesus' twelve disciples
was the brother of John?

    a) Judas Iscariot

    b) Andrew

    c) Matthew

    d) James

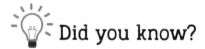 **Did you know?**

Jesus gave James and John a nickname! It
wasn't "The J Brothers"—it was *Boanerges*,
which means "Sons of Thunder."

QUIZ 7

What did Jesus say a wise man builds his house on?

    a) a gold mine

    b) sand

    c) rock

    d) a river bank

Look in the Book: Luke 6:47–48

Double Your Chances: A and B

What did Jesus say a wise man builds his house on?

    a) a gold mine

    b) sand

    c) rock

    d) a river bank

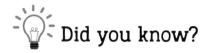 Did you know?

The apostle Paul called Jesus Christ the "spiritual rock" (1 Corinthians 10:4)—so a wise man builds his life on Jesus.

BIBLE BRONZE

What did God give Daniel
the ability to explain?

a) other languages

b) smoke signals

c) dreams

d) the words in rock songs

Look in the Book: Daniel 2:23

Double Your Chances: A and D

What did God give Daniel
the ability to explain?

    a) other languages

    b) smoke signals

    c) dreams

    d) the words in rock songs

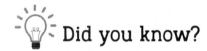 Did you know?

Daniel was also called *Belteshazzar* (Daniel 1:7).

LEVEL 3

What did soldiers put on Jesus' head before His death on the cross?

    a) a helmet

    b) a golden crown

    c) a hood

    d) a crown of thorns

 Look in the Book: Mark 15:16-17

 Double Your Chances: A and C

85

What did soldiers put on Jesus' head before His death on the cross?

    a) a helmet

    b) a golden crown

    c) a hood

    d) a crown of thorns

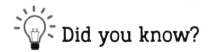 Did you know?

Some prickly bushes are called "Christ's-thorn" plants.

BIBLE SILVER

What city heard Jonah's preaching and turned to God?

  a) Washington, DC

  b) Nineveh

  c) Jerusalem

  d) Rome

Look in the Book: Jonah 3:3-5

Double Your Chances: A and C

What city heard Jonah's preaching and turned to God?

    a) Washington, DC

    b) Nineveh

    c) Jerusalem

    d) Rome

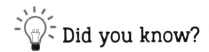 Did you know?

Nineveh was the capital city of an old country called Assyria. If Nineveh were still a city today, it would be part of Iraq.

LEVEL 5

Which of these men did
Jesus heal of blindness?

a) Nicodemus

b) Zacchaeus

c) Bartholomew

d) Bartimaeus

 Look in the Book: Mark 10:46–52

Double Your Chances: A and B

Which of these men did
Jesus heal of blindness?

a) Nicodemus

b) Zacchaeus

c) Bartholomew

d) Bartimaeus

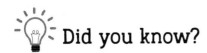 Did you know?

The word "Bar" in a person's name could mean
"the son of." So "Bartimaeus" was "the son of
Timaeus." What would your "Bar" name be?

BIBLE GOLD

What was special about a
man named Enoch?

    a) Jesus raised him from the dead.

    b) He led Israel as a judge.

    c) The apostle Paul healed him of
       blindness.

    d) He never died, because God took
       him straight to heaven.

 Look in the Book: Genesis 5:24

 Double Your Chances: A and B

What was special about a
man named Enoch?

    a) Jesus raised him from the dead.

    b) He led Israel as a judge.

    c) The apostle Paul healed him of
       blindness.

    **d) He never died, because God took
       him straight to heaven.**

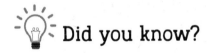 **Did you know?**

Theologians (people whose job is to study
the Bible) call what happened to Enoch
"translation."

QUIZ 8

LEVEL 1

Who gave the five loaves and two fish that Jesus used to feed five thousand people?

     a) Long John Silver

     b) Peter

     c) a little boy

     d) Jesus' mother, Mary

 Look in the Book: John 6:9

 Double Your Chances: A and D

93

Who gave the five loaves and
two fish that Jesus used to
feed five thousand people?

    a) Long John Silver

    b) Peter

    c) a little boy

    d) Jesus' mother, Mary

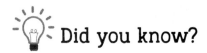 **Did you know?**

Before Jesus handed out food to all the
people, he "gave thanks" (John 6:11). That's
why it's good for *us* to stop and pray before
we eat!

BIBLE BRONZE

What kind of contest did Jacob have with God?

    a) a chess game

    b) a foot race

    c) a wrestling match

    d) a Bible drill

 Look in the Book: Genesis 32:24, 30

Double Your Chances: A and D

What kind of contest did
Jacob have with God?

    a) a chess game

    b) a foot race

    c) a wrestling match

    d) a Bible drill

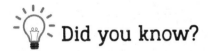 Did you know?

Jacob wrestled with God all night. When they
were done, God changed Jacob's name to
Israel—which means "he struggles with God."

Which of these problems was *not* a plague on Egypt?

    a) chicken pox

    b) frogs

    c) hail

    d) locusts

 Look in the Book: Exodus 8:2, 9:18, 10:4

 Double Your Chances: C and D

Which of these problems was
not a plague on Egypt?

a) chicken pox

b) frogs

c) hail

d) locusts

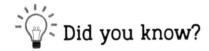 Did you know?

The word *pox* can mean a terrible evil—or a
plague!

BIBLE SILVER

What did Satan tell Jesus
to turn into bread?

     a) a turtle

     b) His sandal

     c) a scroll

     d) a stone

 Look in the Book: Luke 4:3

 Double Your Chances: A and B

What did Satan tell Jesus
to turn into bread?

> a) a turtle
>
> b) His sandal
>
> c) a scroll
>
> **d) a stone**

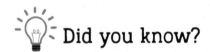 Did you know?

Satan was trying to make Jesus do something wrong—but Jesus never did anything wrong. Jesus fought back with a Bible verse: "Man does not live on bread alone but on every word that comes from the mouth of the LORD" (Deuteronomy 8:3).

LEVEL 5

What had happened to the man who was helped by the Good Samaritan?

    a) He had been struck by lightning.

    b) He had fallen over a cliff.

    c) He had been bitten by a snake.

    d) He had been beaten by robbers.

 Look in the Book: Luke 10:30

 Double Your Chances: A and C

What had happened to the man who was helped by the Good Samaritan?

    a) He had been struck by lightning.

    b) He had fallen over a cliff.

    c) He had been bitten by a snake.

    d) He had been beaten by robbers.

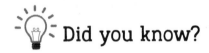 Did you know?

Jesus told the story of the Good Samaritan to explain a verse that says, "Love your neighbor as yourself" (Leviticus 19:18). Jesus was saying that everyone you meet is your neighbor—not just the people who live next door to you.

BIBLE GOLD

Which one of Joseph's brothers kept his other brothers from killing Joseph?

    a) Judah

    b) Benjamin

    c) Dan

    d) Reuben

 Look in the Book: Genesis 37:21

Double Your Chances: A and C

Which one of Joseph's brothers kept his other brothers from killing Joseph?

     a) Judah

     b) Benjamin

     c) Dan

     d) Reuben

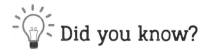 **Did you know?**

Reuben was the oldest of Jacob's twelve sons—the men who started the "twelve tribes of Israel." Genesis 49 will tell you more.

QUIZ 9

LEVEL 1

How many commandments—rules to live by—did God give to Moses?

a) 1

b) 10

c) 25

d) 417

 Look in the Book: Exodus 20:3-17

 Double Your Chances: A and D

How many commandments—rules
to live by—did God give to Moses?

    a) 1

    b) 10

    c) 25

    d) 417

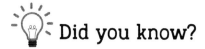 Did you know?

One of the Ten Commandments promises
something good to the person who does it:
"Honor your father and your mother, so that
you may live long in the land the LORD your
God is giving you" (Exodus 20:12).

How long did it take God to create the heavens, the earth, and everything in them?

- a) one second
- b) twenty-four hours
- c) six days
- d) one thousand years

Look in the Book: Genesis 1:31–2:1

 Double Your Chances: A and D

How long did it take God to create the heavens, the earth, and everything in them?

> a) one second

> b) twenty-four hours

> **c) six days**

> d) one thousand years

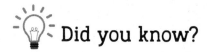 Did you know?

God "saved the best for last" and made people on the sixth day of creation. Then He took the seventh day off and rested.

LEVEL 3

What punishment was allowed
by Pontius Pilate?

a) Jesus' crucifixion

b) John the Baptist's beheading

c) Paul's stay in jail

d) Daniel's night in the lions' den

Look in the Book: Luke 23:23-25

 Double Your Chances: B and C

What punishment was allowed
by Pontius Pilate?

a) Jesus' crucifixion

b) John the Baptist's beheading

c) Paul's stay in jail

d) Daniel's night in the lions' den

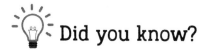 Did you know?

Pontius Pilate's wife told her husband to
leave Jesus alone, because she knew He
was innocent—but Pilate didn't listen to her
(Matthew 27:19–20).

BIBLE SILVER

How old was Abraham when
his son Isaac was born?

  a) 15

  b) 30

  c) 65

  d) 100

Look in the Book: Genesis 21:5

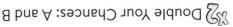
Double Your Chances: A and B

How old was Abraham when his son Isaac was born?

    a) 15

    b) 30

    c) 65

    d) 100

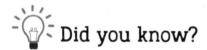 **Did you know?**

Abraham's wife, Sarah, was *ninety* years old when Isaac was born (Genesis 17:17). That's pretty old to be having a baby!

LEVEL 5

What miraculous thing did God use to free Paul and Silas from prison?

    a) a whirlwind

    b) an earthquake

    c) a flash flood

    d) a swarm of locusts

Look in the Book: Acts 16:25-26

Double Your Chances: C and D

What miraculous thing did God use to free Paul and Silas from prison?

    a) a whirlwind

    b) an earthquake

    c) a flash flood

    d) a swarm of locusts

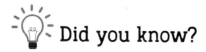 Did you know?

There was an earthquake when Jesus died—Matthew 27:51–52 says, "The earth shook, the rocks split and the tombs broke open. The bodies of many holy people who had died were raised to life." That must have been something to see!

BIBLE GOLD

What was the name of Samuel's mother?

a) Mary Magdalene

b) Ruth

c) Hannah

d) Deborah

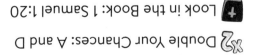

Look in the Book: 1 Samuel 1:20

Double Your Chances: A and D

What was the name of
Samuel's mother?

  a) Mary Magdalene

  b) Ruth

  c) Hannah

  d) Deborah

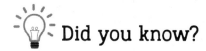 Did you know?

The name *Hannah* is a palindrome—a word
that reads the same way backward or forward.
Here are some others: mom, noon, level. Can
you think of more?

QUIZ 10

LEVEL 1

How does the Bible describe
the tax collector Zacchaeus?

- a) short
- b) handsome
- c) fat
- d) smelly

Look in the Book: Luke 19:3

Double Your Chances: B and D

117

How does the Bible describe
the tax collector Zacchaeus?

a) short

b) handsome

c) fat

d) smelly

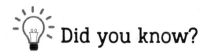 Did you know?

Zacchaeus is one of many "Z" people in the
Bible. There were also Zebedee (the father of
James and John), Zebulun (a son of Jacob),
four Zechariahs (one was the father of John
the Baptist), and Zipporah (Moses' wife), to
name a few.

BIBLE BRONZE

What kind of bush did God use to get Moses' attention?

a) flowering

b) singing

c) burning

d) walking

Look in the Book: Exodus 3:2–3

Double Your Chances: A and B

What kind of bush did God use
to get Moses' attention?

    a) flowering

    b) singing

    c) burning

    d) walking

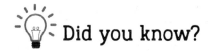 Did you know?

God talked to Moses through the bush—and
said that Moses would lead God's people, the
Israelites, out of their slavery in Egypt. Read
all about it in Exodus 3.

LEVEL 3

What kind of animals was the prodigal son feeding when he decided to go back home?

    a) hamsters

    b) pigs

    c) chickens

    d) cows

 Look in the Book: Luke 15:15-18

 Double Your Chances: A and C

What kind of animals was the prodigal son feeding when he decided to go back home?

a) hamsters

b) pigs

c) chickens

d) cows

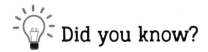 **Did you know?**

The word *prodigal* means "wasteful." So the "prodigal son" was a boy who had wasted the money his father had given him.

BIBLE SILVER

What did God do to the people of Babel to keep them from building their giant tower?

a) He made them go blind.

b) He made them fall asleep.

c) He made them speak other languages.

d) He made them afraid of heights.

 Look in the Book: Genesis 11:8-9

 Double Your Chances: B and D

Kids' Bible Trivia

What did God do to the people
of Babel to keep them from
building their giant tower?

    a) He made them go blind.

    b) He made them fall asleep.

    **c) He made them speak other
       languages.**

    d) He made them afraid of heights.

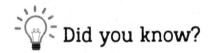 Did you know?

Scientists say there may be more than *three
thousand* different languages in the world
today!

LEVEL 5

What color rope did Rahab put in her window to protect herself and her family?

   a) scarlet

   b) purple

   c) green

   d) periwinkle

 Look in the Book: Joshua 2:21

Double Your Chances: B and D

What color rope did Rahab put
in her window to protect herself
and her family?

a) scarlet

b) purple

c) green

d) periwinkle

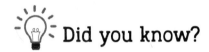 **Did you know?**

Scarlet is a bright red color.

Who did Peter first meet after an angel broke him out of prison?

    a) Lydia

    b) Rhoda

    c) Salome

    d) Julia

Look in the Book: Acts 12:13

Double Your Chances: A and D

Who did Peter first meet after an angel broke him out of prison?

    a) Lydia

    b) Rhoda

    c) Salome

    d) Julia

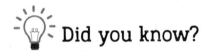 **Did you know?**

The people in Peter's church had been praying hard for Peter, but when Rhoda said Peter was at the door, they didn't believe her. "You're out of your mind," they said (Acts 12:15). They must have forgotten that God answers prayer!

QUIZ 11

LEVEL 1

What did God call Noah's giant boat?

    a) an ark

    b) a bark

    c) a quark

    d) *Titanic*

 Look in the Book: Genesis 6:14

 Double Your Chances: C and D

What did God call Noah's giant boat?

a) an ark

b) a bark

c) a quark

d) *Titanic*

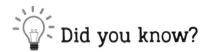 Did you know?

A *bark* is a kind of boat too. . .but a much smaller boat than Noah's!

BIBLE BRONZE

How did four men get into a crowded house and bring their paralyzed friend to Jesus?

    a) They slid down the chimney.

    b) They tunneled through the floor.

    c) They cut through the wall.

    d) They broke through the roof.

 Look in the Book: Mark 2:1–5

 Double Your Chances: A and B

How did four men get into a crowded house and bring their paralyzed friend to Jesus?

    a) They slid down the chimney.

    b) They tunneled through the floor.

    c) They cut through the wall.

    d) They broke through the roof.

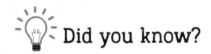 Did you know?

This story happened in Capernaum, the town Jesus lived in after he moved out of Nazareth (Matthew 4:13). Capernaum was on the edge of the Sea of Galilee—where Jesus walked on the water.

LEVEL 3

How were Cain and Abel related?

    a) father and son

    b) brothers

    c) cousins

    d) just third-grade classmates

 Look in the Book: Genesis 4:1–2

 Double Your Chances: A and D

How were Cain and Abel related?

    a) father and son

    b) brothers

    c) cousins

    d) just third-grade classmates

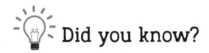 **Did you know?**

Cain was Adam and Eve's first son and the first murderer—because he killed his own brother, Abel. Even today, people who cause trouble are said to be "raising Cain."

What instrument did David play
to make King Saul feel better?

    a) an electric guitar

    b) a harp

    c) a trumpet

    d) a flute

Look in the Book: 1 Samuel 16:23

 Double Your Chances: A and D

What instrument did David play
to make King Saul feel better?

    a) an electric guitar

    b) a harp

    c) a trumpet

    d) a flute

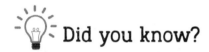 **Did you know?**

God must enjoy harp music too—the book
of Revelation talks three different times
about harps in heaven! Read for yourself in
Revelation 5:8, 14:2, and 15:2.

What kind of seed did Jesus say
the kingdom of heaven was like?

    a) dandelion

    b) mustard

    c) wheat

    d) apple

Look in the Book: Mark 4:30-32

Double Your Chances: A and C

What kind of seed did Jesus say
the kingdom of heaven was like?

    a) dandelion

    b) mustard

    c) wheat

    d) apple

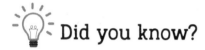 Did you know?

Jesus was saying that His "kingdom," all of the
people who would follow Him, was like a tiny
seed when it started—it was only Jesus and His
twelve disciples. But as they told other people,
and those people told even more people, the
kingdom of heaven grew like a strong tree.
Today, there are millions and millions and
millions of Christians around the world!

BIBLE GOLD

What man "prepared the way" for Jesus?

a) Peter

b) Paul

c) John the Baptist

d) Malachi

 Look in the Book: Matthew 3:1-3

Double Your Chances: A and B

What man "prepared the way" for Jesus?

    a) Peter

    b) Paul

    c) John the Baptist

    d) Malachi

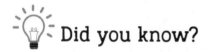 Did you know?

Jesus and John the Baptist were relatives—because their mothers, Mary and Elizabeth, were related (Luke 1:36).

QUIZ 12

LEVEL 1

What people first heard the good news about Jesus' birth from an angel?

- a) fishermen
- b) shepherds
- c) soldiers
- d) TV reporters

 Look in the Book: Luke 2:8-11

 Double Your Chances: C and D

What people first heard the good news about Jesus' birth from an angel?

    a) fishermen

    b) shepherds

    c) soldiers

    d) TV reporters

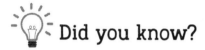 Did you know?

In the song "The First Noel," that begins
    The first noel the angel did say was to
    certain poor shepherds in fields as they lay
noel means "Christmas carol."

BIBLE BRONZE

What did God tell Abraham
to do to his son Isaac?

a) make him eat prunes

b) give him to the priest

c) teach him to play the harp

d) sacrifice him

Look in the Book: Genesis 22:2

Double Your Chances: A and C

What did God tell Abraham
to do to his son Isaac?

    a) make him eat prunes

    b) give him to the priest

    c) teach him to play the harp

    d) sacrifice him

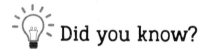 **Did you know?**

Abraham is part of the "Faith Hall of Fame"
in the book of Hebrews. Hebrews 11:19 says
that Abraham was willing to sacrifice Isaac, his
only son, because he believed God would raise
him back to life. God was testing Abraham to
see if he would obey; when Abraham proved
he was willing to obey, God stopped him and
sent a ram to sacrifice instead. Read more in
Genesis 22.

LEVEL 3

What did Peter see inside a
sheet, coming down from
heaven by its four corners?

a) animals, reptiles, and birds

b) gold and silver

c) people of many countries

d) Christmas presents

Look in the Book: Acts 10:9-12

Double Your Chances: B and D

What did Peter see inside a sheet, coming down from heaven by its four corners?

a) animals, reptiles, and birds

b) gold and silver

c) people of many countries

d) Christmas presents

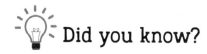 Did you know?

Peter's vision meant that *all* people—should hear the good news about Jesus Christ. The animals Peter saw were "unclean," meaning they were animals that the Jewish people weren't allowed to eat. God told Peter to kill and eat the animals anyway, saying "Do not call anything impure that God has made clean" (Acts 10:15). Peter realized that "God does not show favoritism but accepts from every nation the one who fears him and does what is right" (Acts 10:34–35).

BIBLE SILVER

What were Egypt's kings called?

a) satraps

b) proconsuls

c) pharaohs

d) scary

 Look in the Book: Exodus 5:1–4

x2 Double Your Chances: B and D

What were Egypt's kings called?

    a) satraps

    b) proconsuls

    c) pharaohs

    d) scary

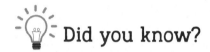 Did you know?

The name *pharaoh* comes from an Egyptian word that means "the royal palace."

LEVEL 5

How long had Lazarus been dead when Jesus brought him back to life?

    a) ten minutes

    b) twelve hours

    c) four days

    d) a year

 Look in the Book: John 11:39-44

Double Your Chances: A and D

How long had Lazarus been dead when Jesus brought him back to life?

    a) ten minutes

    b) twelve hours

    c) four days

    d) a year

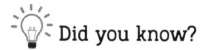 Did you know?

There was another man named Lazarus in the Bible. Check out his story in Luke 16:19–31.

BIBLE GOLD

Who became the leader of
Israel after Moses died?

a) David

b) Joshua

c) Solomon

d) Aaron

 Look in the Book! Numbers 27:18-20

 Double Your Chances: A and C

Who became the leader of
Israel after Moses died?

    a) David

    b) Joshua

    c) Solomon

    d) Aaron

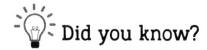 Did you know?

Joshua's name was actually Hoshea, but Moses
changed it (Numbers 13:16). *Joshua* means
"Jehovah [God] is salvation."

QUIZ 13

LEVEL 1

What city's walls fell down in front of Joshua's army?

> a) Jericho
>
> b) Babylon
>
> c) Tyre
>
> d) Los Angeles

 Look in the Book: Joshua 6:2-5

 Double Your Chances: C and D

153

What city's walls fell down in front of Joshua's army?

a) Jericho

b) Babylon

c) Tyre

d) Los Angeles

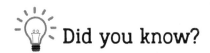 **Did you know?**

Archaeologists (scientists who study people who lived a long time ago) say Jericho is one of the world's oldest cities.

BIBLE BRONZE

What was Samson famous for?

    a) skateboarding skills

    b) great strength

    c) musical talent

    d) writing poems

 Look in the Book: Judges 16:6

 Double Your Chances: A and D

What was Samson famous for?

    a) skateboarding skills

    b) great strength

    c) musical talent

    d) writing poems

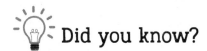 Did you know?

Samson was a judge of Israel for twenty years (Judges 15:20). The judges were the leaders of the country in the days before Israel had a king.

LEVEL 3

What did Jesus turn water into,
as his very first miracle?

a) Mountain Dew

b) blood

c) oil

d) wine

Look in the Book: John 2:1–11

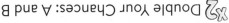
Double Your Chances: A and B

What did Jesus turn water into,
as his very first miracle?

    a) Mountain Dew

    b) blood

    c) oil

    d) wine

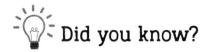 **Did you know?**

Jesus performed this miracle at a wedding.

BIBLE SILVER

What kind of man was the giant Goliath?

    a) a Philadelphian

    b) a Philippian

    c) a Philistine

    d) a philatelist

 Look in the Book: 1 Samuel 17:23

 Double Your Chances: A and D

What kind of man was the giant Goliath?

    a) a Philadelphian

    b) a Philippian

    c) a Philistine

    d) a philatelist

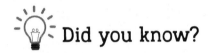 Did you know?

Philistines, Philadelphians, and Philippians were all people from the Bible—but *philatelists* are stamp collectors!

What place did Matthew
leave to follow Jesus?

      a) a butcher's shop

      b) a tax collector's booth

      c) a bakery

      d) a boxing ring

 Look in the Book: Matthew 9:9

 Double Your Chances: C and D

What place did Matthew
leave to follow Jesus?

    a) a butcher's shop

    b) a tax collector's booth

    c) a bakery

    d) a boxing ring

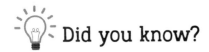 **Did you know?**

Matthew was also called Levi. One time, Levi
invited a bunch of other tax collectors to his
house to have dinner with Jesus. Some people
complained that Jesus was spending His time
with "sinners," but Jesus told them, "It is not
the healthy who need a doctor, but the sick.
I have not come to call the righteous, but
sinners" (Mark 2:17).

BIBLE GOLD

What was the name of Queen Esther's cousin?

a) Mordecai

b) Jeremiah

c) Theophilus

d) Hezekiah

 Look in the Book: Esther 2:7

 Double Your Chances: B and C

What was the name of
Queen Esther's cousin?

a) Mordecai

b) Jeremiah

c) Theophilus

d) Hezekiah

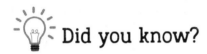 **Did you know?**

Mordecai started a holiday, Purim, that Jewish
people still celebrate each year in February
or March. The holiday remembers Esther's
victory over an evil man named Haman, who
wanted to kill all the Jews. Read more in Esther
9:23–28.

LEVEL 1

Where was Jesus born?

- a) Christmas Island
- b) Beersheba
- c) Jericho
- d) Bethlehem

 Double Your Chances: A and B

 Look in the Book: Matthew 2:1

Where was Jesus born?

   a) Christmas Island

   b) Beersheba

   c) Jericho

   d) Bethlehem

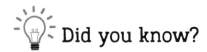 Did you know?

A prophet named Micah said that Jesus would be born in Bethlehem—about seven hundred years before it happened! Here is Micah 5:2: "But you Bethlehem. . .though you are small among the clans of Judah, out of you will come for me one who will be ruler over Israel, whose origins are from of old, from ancient times."

BIBLE BRONZE

What did Jonah do inside the giant fish?

    a) practice karate

    b) pray

    c) cry

    d) build a fire

 Look in the Book: Jonah 2:1

Double Your Chances: A and C

What did Jonah do inside the giant fish?

    a) practice karate

    b) pray

    c) cry

    d) build a fire

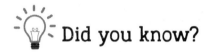 Did you know?

In 1 Thessalonians 5:17, the apostle Paul said we should "pray continually," or all the time—not just if we're stuck inside a big fish!

LEVEL 3

What idol did Moses' brother, Aaron, create for the people of Israel?

    a) the golden bull

    b) the golden eagle

    c) the golden calf

    d) the Golden Arches

Look in the Book: Exodus 32:3-4

Double Your Chances: B and D

What idol did Moses' brother, Aaron, create for the people of Israel?

    a) the golden bull

    b) the golden eagle

    c) the golden calf

    d) the Golden Arches

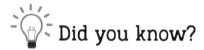 Did you know?

Moses was so mad about this sinful idol that he had the golden calf ground into a powder and sprinkled on the water. Then he made the people of Israel drink the water! Check out the whole story in Exodus 32.

BIBLE SILVER

What was the name of the angel who told Mary she would give birth to Jesus?

a) Michael

b) Zadok

c) Gabriel

d) Hananiah

Double Your Chances: A and B

Look in the Book: Luke 1:26-31

What was the name of the angel who told Mary she would give birth to Jesus?

    a) Michael

    b) Zadok

    c) Gabriel

    d) Hananiah

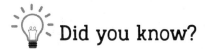 Did you know?

Gabriel also told a couple named Zechariah and Elizabeth that they would have a special son named John the Baptist. Find out more in Luke 1:5–25.

LEVEL 5

What kind of animals helped Samson burn the grain fields of his enemies?

a) lightning bugs

b) lions

c) donkeys

d) foxes

 Look in the Book: Judges 15:3–5

 Double Your Chances: A and C

What kind of animals helped Samson burn the grain fields of his enemies?

    a) lightning bugs

    b) lions

    c) donkeys

    d) foxes

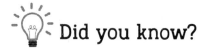 Did you know?

Foxes live in holes in the ground—that's what Jesus said in Matthew 8:20: "Foxes have dens and birds have nests, but the Son of Man has no place to lay his head."

BIBLE GOLD

What does *Golgotha*, the name of the place Jesus was killed on a cross, mean?

   a) The Place of the Dead

   b) The Place of Sadness

   c) The Place of Fear

   d) The Place of the Skull

 Look in the Book: Matthew 27:33

 Double Your Chances: A and C

What does *Golgotha*, the name of the place Jesus was killed on a cross, mean?

    a) The Place of the Dead

    b) The Place of Sadness

    c) The Place of Fear

    d) The Place of the Skull

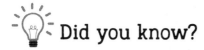 Did you know?

When Jesus was on the cross, the sun went dark for three hours—from noon until 3 p.m. (Luke 23:44–45). Do you think that might have caught some people's attention? Even one of the Roman soldiers who was guarding Jesus said, "Surely this was a righteous man" (Luke 23:47).

QUIZ 15

LEVEL 1

How did Moses and the people of Israel cross the Red Sea?

    a) in an airplane

    b) in boats

    c) they swam

    d) they walked across on dry land

 Look in the Book: Exodus 14:21–22

 Double Your Chances: A and B

How did Moses and the people
of Israel cross the Red Sea?

    a) in an airplane

    b) in boats

    c) they swam

    d) they walked across on dry land

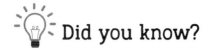 **Did you know?**

This wasn't the only time the people of Israel
walked across a body of water on dry ground.
Joshua once led the people across the Jordan
River the same way (Joshua 3:13–17).

Where did Jesus say we should store our treasure?

a) in heaven

b) in a bank

c) in a cave

d) in a pirate's chest

 Look in the Book: Matthew 6:20

 Double Your Chances: B and D

Where did Jesus say we should store our treasure?

a) in heaven

b) in a bank

c) in a cave

d) in a pirate's chest

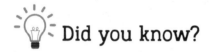 Did you know?

The apostle Paul told people *how* to store up treasure in heaven: "Command them to do good, to be rich in good deeds, and to be generous and willing to share. In this way they will lay up treasure for themselves as a firm foundation for the coming age" (1 Timothy 6:18–19).

Who had a dream about angels going up and down a ladder to heaven?

    a) Noah

    b) Jacob

    c) Daniel

    d) Habakkuk

 Look in the Book: Genesis 28:10–12

x2 Double Your Chances: C and D

Who had a dream about angels going up and down a ladder to heaven?

    a) Noah

    b) Jacob

    c) Daniel

    d) Habakkuk

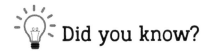 Did you know?

African-American slaves used this story to make up a song—called a "spiritual"—that went like this:

> We are climbing Jacob's ladder,
> we are climbing Jacob's ladder,
> we are climbing Jacob's ladder,
> soldiers of the cross.

BIBLE SILVER

Why did Jesus use a whip to drive people out of the temple?

a) They were making too much noise.

b) They were using God's house as a marketplace.

c) They were drinking wine.

d) They were drawing pictures on their bulletins.

 Look in the Book: John 2:13-16

Double Your Chances: A and D

Why did Jesus use a whip to drive people out of the temple?

   a) They were making too much noise.

   b) They were using God's house as a marketplace.

   c) They were drinking wine.

   d) They were drawing pictures on their bulletins.

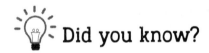 Did you know?

When the disciples saw Jesus chase the sellers out of the temple, they remembered a verse from the Psalms: "Zeal for your house consumes me" (Psalm 69:9). That meant Jesus' concern about the temple "ate Him up."

LEVEL 5

What was Esau really good at doing?

   a) hunting

   b) swimming

   c) woodworking

   d) rodeo riding

Look in the Book: Genesis 25:27

Double Your Chances: C and D

What was Esau really good at doing?

    a) hunting

    b) swimming

    c) woodworking

    d) rodeo riding

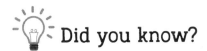 **Did you know?**

The Bible talks about two other men who were good at hunting: Ishmael, a son of Abraham, who "lived in the desert and became an archer" (Genesis 21:20), and Nimrod, "a mighty hunter before the LORD" (Genesis 10:9).

BIBLE GOLD

What couple died after lying to Peter about an offering they made?

    a) Hosea and Gomer

    b) Aquila and Priscilla

    c) Ananias and Sapphira

    d) Ruth and Boaz

 Look in the Book: Acts 5:1-10

 Double Your Chances: B and D

What couple died after lying to Peter about an offering they made?

  a) Hosea and Gomer

  b) Aquila and Priscilla

  c) Ananias and Sapphira

  d) Ruth and Boaz

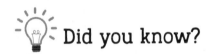 Did you know?

The deaths of Ananias and Sapphira put a real scare into the people who knew them. In Acts 5:11, Luke says, "Great fear seized the whole church and all who heard about these events."

QUIZ 16

What kind of animal tempted Eve to eat the fruit that God said she should not eat?

a) serpent

b) hawk

c) horse

d) hippopotamus

 Look in the Book: Genesis 3:1–5

 Double Your Chances: B and D

189

What kind of animal tempted
Eve to eat the fruit that God
said she should not eat?

    a) serpent

    b) hawk

    c) horse

    d) hippopotamus

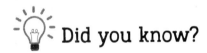 **Did you know?**

Many people think that the fruit Adam and
Eve ate was an apple—but the Bible doesn't
say that. The fruit came from "the tree of
the knowledge of good and evil" (Genesis
2:17), and nobody knows what that tree's fruit
looks like!

BIBLE BRONZE

What fancy piece of clothing did
Joseph receive from his father, Jacob?

- a) a robe
- b) a hat
- c) a belt
- d) a necktie

 Look in the Book: Genesis 37:3

 Double Your Chances: B and D

What fancy piece of clothing did
Joseph receive from his father, Jacob?

    a) a robe

    b) a hat

    c) a belt

    d) a necktie

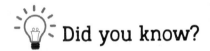 **Did you know?**

Joseph was the second youngest of Jacob's
twelve sons—and he was Daddy's favorite. Joseph's ten older brothers hated him
because of that, and actually thought about
killing Joseph. In the end, they sold him as
a slave—but that turned out to be a good
thing. The whole story is in the last fourteen
chapters of Genesis.

How did God take Elijah up to heaven?

a) in a hot air balloon

b) on the arm of an angel

c) in a whirlwind

d) on the back of an eagle

Look in the Book: 2 Kings 2:11

Double Your Chances: A and D

How did God take Elijah up to heaven?

>   a) in a hot air balloon
>
>   b) on the arm of an angel
>
>   **c) in a whirlwind**
>
>   d) on the back of an eagle

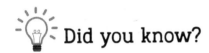 Did you know?

A prophet called Nahum once wrote about God's power, saying that "His way is in the whirlwind and the storm, and clouds are the dust of his feet" (Nahum 1:3). But Nahum also said that "The LORD is good, a refuge in times of trouble. He cares for those who trust in him" (Nahum 1:7).

BIBLE SILVER

How many of the ten lepers that Jesus healed remembered to thank God?

    a) all ten

    b) nine

    c) only one

    d) none

 Look in the Book: Luke 17:12-19

 Double Your Chances: A and D

How many of the ten lepers that Jesus healed remembered to thank God?

    a) all ten

    b) nine

    c) only one

    d) none

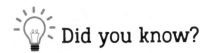 Did you know?

The apostle Paul said we should be thankful all the time—for good things and even for the not-so-good things—because "this is God's will for you in Christ Jesus" (1 Thessalonians 5:18).

LEVEL 5

What color cloth was sold by Lydia, who became a Christian after hearing Paul's preaching?

- a) red
- b) blue
- c) brown
- d) purple

Look in the Book: Acts 16:14

Double Your Chances: B and C

What color cloth was sold by
Lydia, who became a Christian
after hearing Paul's preaching?

> a) red
>
> b) blue
>
> c) brown
>
> **d) purple**

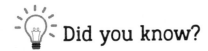 Did you know?

In Bible times, people who wore purple
clothes were often the rich and powerful.
Remember Mordecai in the story of Esther?
When he pleased the king, he was given "royal
garments [clothes] of blue and white, a large
crown of gold and a purple robe of fine linen"
(Esther 8:15).

rom what dangerous place
id God rescue Shadrach,
Meshach, and Abednego?

a) a rushing river

b) a fiery furnace

c) a collapsing cave

d) a teetering treehouse

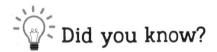 Did you know?

Shadrach, Meshach, and Abednego were all
friends of Daniel—the guy who spent a night
in the lions' den. They all lived together while
they served the king of Babylon (Daniel 2:17).

What was Saul looking for
when he learned he would
become the king of Israel?

a) a wife

b) lost donkeys

c) water

d) a job

Look in the Book! 1 Samuel 10:1–2

Double Your Chances: A and D

What was Saul looking for when he learned he would become the king of Israel?

  a) a wife

  b) lost donkeys

  c) water

  d) a job

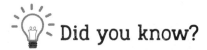 **Did you know?**

One time, Jesus told a story about lost *sheep*—saying that a shepherd with one hundred sheep would leave ninety-nine of them to go find the one that had wandered away. He was saying that God goes out of His way to look for us, and make us part of His family. Read more in Matthew 18:10–14.

LEVEL 1

From what dangerous place did God rescue Shadrach, Meshach, and Abednego?

  a) a rushing river

  b) a fiery furnace

  c) a collapsing cave

  d) a teetering treehouse

Look in the Book: Daniel 3:26-28

Double Your Chances: C and D

BIBLE BRONZE

Who named all of the animals?

a) God

b) Adam

c) Noah

d) Zack the Zookeeper

Look in the Book: Genesis 2:19

Double Your Chances: A and D

Who named all of the animals?

    a) God

    b) Adam

    c) Noah

    d) Zack the Zookeeper

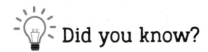 **Did you know?**

Adam named all the animals just before God gave him Eve as his wife. As nice as the animals were, none of them was a "suitable helper" for Adam (Genesis 2:20). So, before long, God made Adam fall into a deep sleep, took a rib from his side, and formed Eve to be Adam's wife.

LEVEL 3

What did Jesus say little children should do?

    a) "Be quiet in church!"

    b) "Come to me."

    c) "Read your Bibles."

    d) "Obey your parents."

 Look in the Book: Matthew 19:14

Double Your Chances: A and C

What did Jesus say little children should do?

> a) "Be quiet in church!"
>
> **b) "Come to me."**
>
> c) "Read your Bibles."
>
> d) "Obey your parents."

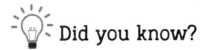 **Did you know?**

The song "Jesus Loves Me," which talks a lot about little children and Jesus, is more than 150 years old! The first verse of the song was written in 1860, just before the American Civil War.

BIBLE SILVER

What kind of birds fed the prophet Elijah when he was hiding from King Ahab?

a) eagles

b) storks

c) hummingbirds

d) ravens

Look in the Book: 1 Kings 17:1-3

Double Your Chances: B and C

What kind of birds fed the prophet Elijah when he was hiding from King Ahab?

  a) eagles

  b) storks

  c) hummingbirds

  d) ravens

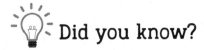 Did you know?

Jesus once talked about ravens, saying, "They do not sow or reap, they have no storeroom or barn; yet God feeds them" (Luke 12:24). Then Jesus said, "And how much more valuable you are than birds!"

Double Your Chances: A and B

Look in the Book: John 19:19

QUIZ 17

LEVEL 5

What did the sign on the cross say that Jesus was King of?

a) the heavens

b) the world

c) the Jews

d) the universe

What did the sign on the cross
say that Jesus was king of?

    a) the heavens

    b) the world

    c) the Jews

    d) the universe

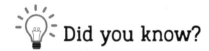 Did you know?

In Revelation 19:16, Jesus is called "KING OF
KINGS AND LORD OF LORDS"—it's even written on
His clothes!

BIBLE GOLD

What king had Daniel thrown
into the lions' den?

a) Darius

b) Nebuchadnezzar

c) Ahab

d) Herod

 Look in the Book: Daniel 6:16–25

 Double Your Chances: B and D

What king had Daniel thrown into the lions' den?

a) Darius

b) Nebuchadnezzar

c) Ahab

d) Herod

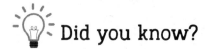 Did you know?

King Darius really liked Daniel, and felt terrible putting him into the lions' den. Darius had been tricked into passing a law that said everyone should pray to him—but when Daniel kept praying to God, the king couldn't change the law, and Daniel had to spend a night with the lions. The good news is that Daniel came out just fine—"My God sent his angel, and he shut the mouths of the lions," Daniel said. "They have not hurt me" (Daniel 6:22). Read the whole story in Daniel 6.

LEVEL 1

Where did Adam and Eve live until God made them move out?

    a) the mountain of Eden

    b) the valley of Eden

    c) the Garden of Eden

    d) the hotel of Eden

 Look in the Book: Genesis 2:8

x2 Double Your Chances: A and D

Where did Adam and Eve live until God made them move out?

    a) the mountain of Eden

    b) the valley of Eden

    c) the Garden of Eden

    d) the hotel of Eden

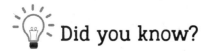 Did you know?

After Adam and Eve had to leave the Garden of Eden, angels and a flaming sword kept them out (Genesis 3:24).

BIBLE BRONZE

What job did King David have
when he was just a boy?

  a) shepherd

  b) baker

  c) carpenter

  d) lawn mower

ƐƖ–ƖƖ:9Ɩ lǝnɯɐS Ɩ :ʞoo𝗕 ǝɥʇ uᴉ ʞ oo˥

◻ puɐ 𝗕 :sǝɔuɐɥƆ ɹno⅄ ǝlqnoᗡ

What job did King David have
when he was just a boy?

   a) shepherd

   b) baker

   c) carpenter

   d) lawn mower

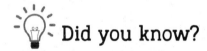 Did you know?

Later in his life, David wrote the famous words
of Psalm 23: "The LORD is my shepherd. . . ."

QUIZ 18

LEVEL 3

Where did baby Moses' mother hide
a basket holding her little boy?

a) in the Nile River

b) in a tree top

c) in a cave

d) in the trunk of her car

Look in the Book: Exodus 2:3

Double Your Chances: B and D

Where did baby Moses' mother hide
a basket holding her little boy?

a) in the Nile River

b) in a tree top

c) in a cave

d) in the trunk of her car

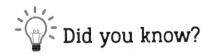 **Did you know?**

The Nile is the longest river in the world—
more than 4,100 miles long!

How did Jesus calm a storm on the sea?

    a) He spoke to the storm.

    b) He touched the water with a stick.

    c) He waved His arms over the sea.

    d) He dipped His robe into the water.

 Look in the Book: Mark 4:39

 Double Your Chances: B and C

How did Jesus calm a storm on the sea?

a) **He spoke to the storm.**

b) He touched the water with a stick.

c) He waved His arms over the sea.

d) He dipped His robe into the water.

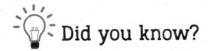 Did you know?

Psalm 107 says that God both starts and stops the storm! "For he spoke and stirred up a tempest [storm] that lifted high the waves" (verse 25); later, God "stilled the storm to a whisper; the waves of the sea were hushed" (verse 29).

LEVEL 5

What kind of animal did God give Abraham to sacrifice, instead of his son Isaac?

      a) a bull

      b) a sparrow

      c) a lamb

      d) a ram

 Look in the Book: Genesis 22:13-14

 Double Your Chances: B and C

What kind of animal did God give Abraham to sacrifice, instead of his son Isaac?

a) a bull

b) a sparrow

c) a lamb

d) a ram

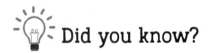 Did you know?

Rams are like sheep, but have big curved horns on their heads.

BIBLE GOLD

Who was Rachel's older sister,
who also married Jacob?

  a) Leah

  b) Deborah

  c) Salome

  d) Phoebe

 Look in the Book: Genesis 29:25-27

 Double Your Chances: C and D

Who was Rachel's older sister,
who also married Jacob?

    a) Leah

    b) Deborah

    c) Salome

    d) Phoebe

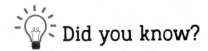 Did you know?

Rachel and Leah's father tricked Jacob into
marrying *both* girls—even though Jacob really
loved Rachel (Genesis 29:14–30). When Jacob
showed more love to Rachel than to Leah, it
caused a lot of problems in the family. Later,
Jacob would cause more problems by choosing
a favorite son—by loving Joseph more than his
eleven other boys.

QUIZ 19

LEVEL 1

What weapon did David use to knock down the giant Goliath?

    a) a machine gun

    b) a bow and arrow

    c) a spear

    d) a sling

 Look in the Book! 1 Samuel 17:49-50

 Double Your Chances: A and C

What weapon did David use to knock down the giant Goliath?

    a) a machine gun

    b) a bow and arrow

    c) a spear

    d) a sling

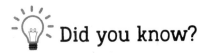 Did you know?

David had five stones to use in his sling (1 Samuel 17:40)—but he only needed one (verses 48–50)!

QUIZ 19

BIBLE BRONZE

Which disciple walked on
water with Jesus?

a) Philip

b) Matthew

c) Thomas

d) Peter

Look in the Book: Matthew 14:29

Double Your Chances: A and C

227

Which disciple walked on
water with Jesus?

    a) Philip

    b) Matthew

    c) Thomas

    d) Peter

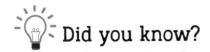 Did you know?

Peter could be very brave—from the time he
walked on the water to the time he fought
to protect Jesus. On the night Jesus was
arrested, Peter grabbed a sword and hit a
man named Malchus, cutting off his ear (John
18:10). Lucky for Malchus, Jesus healed him
right away (Luke 22:50–51).

How did Delilah make Samson weak?

    a) She got him drunk.

    b) She had his head shaved.

    c) She poisoned his food.

    d) She gave him a big kiss.

Look in the Book: Judges 16:18-19

Double Your Chances: A and D

How did Delilah make Samson weak?

    a) She got him drunk.

    b) She had his head shaved.

    c) She poisoned his food.

    d) She gave him a big kiss.

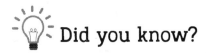 **Did you know?**

Samson was called a "Nazirite"—a person who served God in special ways. The Nazirite rules said that Samson should never cut his hair (Judges 13:5). When his head was shaved, Samson lost the strength God had given him.

BIBLE SILVER

What did Esau sell to his brother
Jacob for a bowl of stew?

    a) his birthplace

    b) his birthright

    c) his birthstone

    d) his birth certificate

 Look in the Book: Genesis 25:29–34

 Double Your Chances: A and C

What did Esau sell to his brother
Jacob for a bowl of stew?

   a) his birthplace

   b) his birthright

   c) his birthstone

   d) his birth certificate

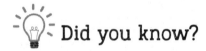 Did you know?

The birthright was a blessing especially for the
oldest son in a family. One king of Judah, a
man named Jehoshaphat, gave his sons "many
gifts of silver and gold and articles of value,
as well as fortified cities in Judah, but he had
given the kingdom to Jehoram because he
was his firstborn son" (2 Chronicles 21:3).

LEVEL 5

How many days did Jesus fast—
go without eating—while the
devil was tempting Him?

     a) 1

     b) 12

     c) 40

     d) 365

 Look in the Book: Luke 4:1–2

 Double Your Chances: A and D

How many days did Jesus fast—
go without eating—while the
devil was tempting Him?

     a) 1

     b) 12

     c) 40

     d) 365

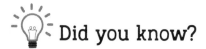 **Did you know?**

Moses fasted forty days too—when God was
giving him the Ten Commandments on Mount
Sinai (Exodus 34:28).

BIBLE GOLD

What did the mother of James and John once ask Jesus?

a) that her sons would never die

b) that her sons could sit at Jesus' side in heaven

c) that her sons could turn stones into gold

d) that her sons would have many children

 Look in the Book: Matthew 20:21

 Double Your Chances: A and C

What did the mother of James
and John once ask Jesus?

a) that her sons would never die

**b) that her sons could sit at Jesus'
side in heaven**

c) that her sons could turn stones
into gold

d) that her sons would have many
children

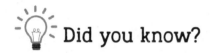 **Did you know?**

The other disciples got mad when they heard
what James and John's mother asked—so
Jesus taught them about how to be *really*
important. "Whoever wants to become great
among you," Jesus said, "must be your ser-
vant" (Matthew 20:26). Jesus reminded the
disciples that He hadn't come to earth for
people to serve Him, but so that He could
serve others—"and to give his life as a ransom
for many" (Matthew 20:28).

QUIZ 20

LEVEL 1

What kind of bird called out after Peter denied Jesus the third time?

    a) a rooster

    b) an eagle

    c) a blue jay

    d) a killdeer

 Look in the Book: Matthew 26:73-75

x2) Double Your Chances: A and B

What kind of bird called out after Peter denied Jesus the third time?

a) a rooster

b) an eagle

c) a blue jay

d) a killdeer

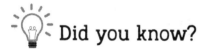 **Did you know?**

Jesus knew ahead of time that Peter would say he didn't even know Jesus (look at Matthew 26:33–34). After Peter denied Jesus, he remembered what Jesus had said— and Peter felt so bad that he began to cry (Matthew 26:75).

BIBLE BRONZE

What did God put in the sky as a promise never again to destroy the earth with a flood?

a) birds

b) the moon

c) a rainbow

d) fighter jets

Look in the Book: Genesis 9:13-16

Double Your Chances: A and D

What did God put in the sky as a promise never again to destroy the earth with a flood?

    a) birds

    b) the moon

    c) a rainbow

    d) fighter jets

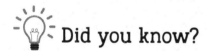 Did you know?

There's a rainbow above God's throne in heaven! See for yourself in Ezekiel 1:28 and Revelation 4:3.

LEVEL 3

What kind of bug does Proverbs say
is an example for lazy people?

  a) jitterbug

  b) moth

  c) grasshopper

  d) ant

  Look in the Book: Proverbs 6:6-8

  Double Your Chances: A and C

What kind of bug does Proverbs say is an example for lazy people?

    a) jitterbug

    b) moth

    c) grasshopper

    d) ant

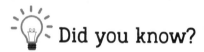 **Did you know?**

Some ants are just like farmers! One kind of ant chews up green leaves to make a "garden" that grows fungus to eat. Another kind of ant keeps a bug called an aphid like human farmers keep a cow—and drinks the juice the aphid makes.

BIBLE SILVER

Why did King Xerxes choose a girl named Esther to be his queen?

 a) She was smart.

 b) She was beautiful.

 c) She was rich.

 d) She was a good cook.

 Look in the Book: Esther 2:17

 Double Your Chances: C and D

Why did King Xerxes choose a girl named Esther to be his queen?

 a) She was smart.

 b) She was beautiful.

 c) She was rich.

 d) She was a good cook.

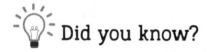 Did you know?

Esther also had another name—Hadassah (Esther 2:7).

How did Jesus go up to heaven forty days after He came back to life from the dead?

    a) on the arm of an angel

    b) in a cloud

    c) in a golden chariot

    d) on the wings of an eagle

 Look in the Book: Acts 1:9

 Double Your Chances: A and D

How did Jesus go up to heaven
forty days after He came back
to life from the dead?

    a) on the arm of an angel

    b) in a cloud

    c) in a golden chariot

    d) on the wings of an eagle

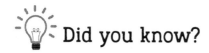 Did you know?

Jesus will come back to earth again in the
same way! Angels told the people who
watched Jesus go up to heaven that He would
"come back in the same way" (Acts 1:11). And
Jesus Himself once said, "You will see the Son
of Man [Jesus]. . .coming on the clouds of
heaven" (Matthew 26:64).

BIBLE GOLD

What sin had Moses committed when he was a young man in Egypt?

    a) He had called Pharaoh a bad name.

    b) He had killed an Egyptian.

    c) He had stolen Pharaoh's money.

    d) He had lied to his mother.

Look in the Book: Exodus 2:11-12

Double Your Chances: A and D

What sin had Moses committed when he was a young man in Egypt?

    a) He had called Pharaoh a bad name.

    b) He had killed an Egyptian.

    c) He had stolen Pharaoh's money.

    d) He had lied to his mother.

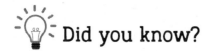 **Did you know?**

Moses was the adopted grandson of the Egyptian pharaoh—because the pharaoh's daughter made Moses her son after she found him in a basket in the Nile River (Exodus 2:9).

SO HOW DID YOU DO?

We hope you answered a lot of questions right and enjoyed your time with *Kids' Bible Trivia*!

But even if you didn't know everything, that's okay. Keep reading and studying your Bible. Learning God's Word is a process that continues throughout your whole life.

And be sure you're not learning just to be able to answer Bible trivia questions. . .learn God's Word to really know God, through His Son, Jesus Christ.

That's the most important thing you'll ever learn from the Bible!

That's in the Bible?

Let's face it—the Bible contains some weird and wacky stuff! This book, written especially for 8–12-year-olds, contains over 800 fun and fascinating entries on people, places, events, and ideas of scripture, with special features on the unusual (and sometimes *gross*) things to keep you turning the pages.

Paperback / 978-1-64352-709-3